You must not hop on pop.

D0331240

You must not hop on pop.

TM & copyright © by Dr. Seuss Enterprises, L.P. 2019

Published in the United States by Random House Children's Books,
a division of Penguin Random House LLC, New York.
The artwork that appears herein was first published in various books by Dr. Seuss.

Random House and the colophon are registered trademarks of Penguin Random House LLC.

Visit us on the Web!
Seussville.com
rhcbooks.com

Educators and librarians, for a variety of teaching tools, visit us at
RHTeachersLibrarians.com

ISBN 978-1-9848-4812-3

MANUFACTURED IN CHINA   10 9 8 7 6 5 4 3 2 1   First Edition

Random House Children's Books supports the First Amendment
and celebrates the right to read.

Dr. Seuss's
I Love

POP!

A Celebration of DADS

Random House  New York

I love you, **POP**!
You are **CARING**.

You are BRAVE.

You are SMART.

You are **FUNNY**.

In good times . . .

And in bad times . . .

You are always my
biggest supporter.

Even when I get
carried away . . .

Or make
too much noise . . .

Or bring home
strange friends...

Or ignore
your advice . . .

You still **LOVE** me.

And that is why
I **LOVE** you, **POP**!

You must not hop on pop.

You must not hop on pop.